A Mirror Completes a Home

A Mirror Completes a Home

Melanie Grace

Grace Collective Press

For my inner child and the child within all of us.

For Kelly, thank you for helping me make peace.

For Blake, thank you for sharing your healing heart.

To my parents, thank you for your understanding.

For Annabelle, may you finally find forgiveness,
closure, and freedom.

home is where the heart is
at least that's what they say
if I pack my bags and come over
would you let me stay
decorate your plaster with sweet nothings
frame my love for you to always see
open the blinds hiding any light
mending a home into what it should be
another's baggage
yet more space to roam
for a mirror completes a home

a light goes out in her heart
when second guessing herself
becomes a habit
she forgets that he made her laugh
yet still tries to remind herself
every day
light at the end of the tunnel
sunshine after the rain
peace is what she's been searching for
without having to jump through hoops
or needing to be saved
she's the mother and the child
but the child has been afraid

I think we broke the spell last night
on a night of shooting stars
beaming from the earth itself
my cheeks have remained rosey
laid in my glass coffin
barely breathing
you see my life
even through closed eyes
two stars in each other's orbit
was it my fault for waiting so long
with a lover who left me
loving on my own
i'm no longer that lonely widow and nun
the curse of loving unconditionally
blessed me with beautiful love
my noble lover never came back
going back on his word
but now i'm stargazing at constellations
within the freckles around your eyes
and for once the universe
makes a little more sense

let me guide you
with the sureness of my heart
four green eyes
two parallel lines
separate lives intertwined
afraid from the start
in fear of an uncharted race
it's this dissonance we face
taking these roads less traveled
strengthening hearts already strong
no blindfolds on
we turn this dissonance into song
four green eyes grasping what is beyond
two parallel lines redrawn
redrawn as one

cicadas in the summertime
fresh mulch on the lawn
the child within me is grieving
facing the harsh consequences
of over giving
do I dare accept healthy love
maybe I could've loved you
maybe I did
but you would never let me
every day
dawn strikes down the illusion
every night
the clock strikes twelve
and my life built around you unwinds
mirror in the sky
heaven up above
what is love
the grandfather clock of time won't tell me
love has boundaries
but no walls
the child within me
deserves to be free
free to lay in the grass
and feel nurturing love again
she deserves to receive love
without having to prove
without having to search and find

my shadow

my muse

my waking thought

fuel for my survival

fused to my heart

two flames eternal

set my soul on fire

bring water to the heat without rival

stillness brought to life

life frozen in sweet surrender

sanctuary to be held in your kind eyes

such a grand thing

just one person could bring

a cracked door
never mended my heart
the way the warmth of your openness does
there's a woody scent in the room
and you're playing a nineties tune
I hate those red plates
but I think i'm sticking with you
suddenly I forget how to speak
when you say you love me
I forget that i'm not the only one
responsible for making a home
closure didn't give me what I was looking for
now i'm slowly relearning
to trust in another's truth

a world with no more night
an everlasting flower bloom
lead me away from my solitude
to grow in years and time
yet bask in a never ending youth

the boy said

wait for me

the man said

i've been waiting for you

I sent a letter to both

saying I would be waiting

under the crape myrtle tree

somewhere out there

the angels knew

I couldn't spend another summer

in the cold

the man beat me to the tree

there he was suspended by one leg

with arms behind his back

by choice

not bound

he's realized love is not possession

and that his mirror won't wait

truth needs expression

was the reflection an illusion

all of these things you will have learned

too late

I do not wish to spend my life longing

my days have never felt so long and full

that's a choice i've made

at fates expense
is it ever a coincidence
feels like a hinderance
is it my own doing
my own contract
cursive letters scribbled so hastily
the expense of fate
do I dare wait
for the next luck of the draw
or lack thereof
the harsh snap of two triangle blades
would maybe feel more gentle in my hands

the house of cards may tumble
but the cards still exist
endless options
limitless
let's build them up together
if they fall this time
we can laugh
and blame it on the wind
it's never the end

what is peace
declaration of certainty
on a piece of paper
disconnected from its genesis
true intention
lost so long ago
the mass of a tree
lies beneath what we can see
what we can comprehend
is true peace
the bittersweet simplicity
of a forest ablaze by a change in draft
fearful words unprovoked
calmed by compassion
tact in the midst of confusion
promising scarcely the certainty
that the other will never
be alone in their fear
because there is no knowing
the lie we have assigned peace
peace can only truly grow
as the roots of trees stay below
through finding another
to share your walk through the unknown

rainbows are a reminder
that the same pain
never happens twice
a loophole
to the permanence
and transience of life

i'm tired of takers
blood on my hands
from carving this path
never safe knowing where we stand
letting the blood leave a trail anyways
because when I first looked into those eyes
I saw deep love
a dry desert has become your mouth
every word bleeding lack
lack of love for oneself
lack of compassion for another
lack of truth and integrity
lack being the real answer
the realization never realized
beyond your eyes
always looking at me as if I was in disguise
a clone of the past
when I am a new heart
a heart not built to be owned
or loaned
or borrowed
a heart with intention to last
spread thin i've become
so accustomed to skinny love
you built shelter in this dry desert
and i'm crossing the moon river to build a home

he thought it was witchcraft
but it was only a divine woman's love and wrath

i've been struck many times
with boys who cry wolf
at first I believe in their tales
because I love a good story
boys who live in the land
between two towers
between dog and wolf
the magnetism of a little glimpse
of shining light so far away
their story is a call
for the next muse in line
next time you start spinning
be sure to leave a trail
hold on to your reality
because he's as constant as a star in the night sky
barely glowing in the growing darkness
and will not be there when you fall

bird in a cage
trying to keep me safe
a safe distant fantasy
always at arm's length
to keep your heart out of harm's way
don't you see
you have me
with doors open I stay

a vision in the waiting room
feels like waiting is all I ever do
I only get angry because I miss you
and I only hate you when you're not being true

what I am most sorry for
above everything else
is that no amount
of poems and music
proclamations of truth
metaphors of the soul
sweet nothings
could ever express
the feeling you give me
the way you make my heart sing

hold me like a guitar
fingers gentle on my strings
gentle but strong with the way you sing
like a wave
washing away everything
the sound of fear from long ago
replaced with a song only we know
a song we've wrote
learning two makes a harmony
when we're gentle on the strings

sirens and ghosts
withhold me from sleep
my mind dances to a place
where your arms are around me
the beat of your heart
keeping me safe

lonesome chess piece
you wait in your square
my scream shakes the board
I need you to know I care
i'm there i'm there
tell you everyday
you're never far away
need to know you're here to stay
I shake the board until you fall
never mean to
worried that if I don't
you'll move nowhere at all

I don't know what to do
not used to holding someone
as irreplaceable as you
feels like something to lose
a prized possession
too valuable to use

nothing I don't like
about those shimmering green eyes
everything I don't like
I find some sense of duality lies
your sullen intensity
your cool facade
i need to break down
calms me for now
a rock in theory
an iceberg in reality
will I ever know the depth
within the sycamore forest of your mind
can you be the shelter I need
or will you always be in disguise
one day you had told me
to text you anytime I want
and I want to all the time

pretty and nuanced
those words linger in my mind
pretty and nuanced
a painting in a museum
untouchable
filled with a depth
too complex
to ruminate upon
beyond an initial glance
I wish to be hung on the plaster
of someone's humble wall
captivating it's owner in a trance
invested in knowing nuances hidden within
not because they need to know
or I need them to know
done in admiration
done just because they wanted so

you cannot rush art
nor can you force a flower to grow
water and sun will facilitate
but do nothing beyond anticipate
accustomed to showing up as an artist
at best birthing a sketch
the connection we share is the greatest masterpiece
in which I envision untethered by time
but i'm used to having to rush
and tightly hold onto my brush
but you cannot rush art
nor can you force a flower to grow

I once was a very lovely
very frightened girl
accustomed to barren land
chained to the tower
no difference outside or within
looking in your eyes I forget it's there
I no longer care
what lingers on the roof
or that is concealed
behind obscure doors
with you I spread my wings
wings that carry me beyond where
a very frightened girl could have dreamed
steady as the heron
I follow the moon river
knowing it leads me
to a soft and bountiful place to land

how do I know how you feel
I am gifted and I am cursed
my angel of music
the chant of your song in my soul
your truth my favorite verse
scared to be touched yet dying to be
i'll give you my hand to hold
in the depths of your longing trance
my soul yearns for you to take a chance

wishful thinking
something on my chest
trying to confess
probability is uncertainty
so why do I count on the worst
when I could hope for the best
everytime i wish for my death
I change and regret
expectations make me a mess

hypothetical

I fell in love with a hypothetical
a love of an ignorant bliss
taught by the propaganda of true loves kiss
I stare in the mirror and proclaim it is you
with visions of a fantasy just out of view
a pedestal will not fit anyone but me
and yet you had me begging on my knees
hypothetical love is all that you were
so now I will continue to love me first

freedom at last
no more believing in the past
i'm riding my broomstick
into the fifth dimension
where I have a full love waiting
one who stays true
one who looks in the mirror
one who doesn't paint me as a danger
for reflecting on silly things like dreams
they seemed to serve purpose
when the dreams boosted ego
it changed the day I decided not to stay the same
when I dreamt I was a phoenix
who lost her wings
I didn't realize whose hands held the shears
my greatest fear was walking away
I thought that was being on the same page
but next thing I knew
I was all alone on the ground
still without wings
I got so sad
life felt limited living in a cloud of contradictions
isolation of slow and subtle manipulation
and I still could never point the finger of blame
my wings will grow from hope
hope that love still has power over shame

my moon
what would I do without you
light to guide me through darkness
transform it into something to use
in a night never turning
you make that night a home
learning it's okay to be alone
alone an illusion
because in the light there's you
standing in an open doorway
open arms
emotions free to roam

embraced in a hug
you stab me with a knife
exposing a wound caused by another life
arms wide open for you
i'm turned into prey
hoping you would preserve yourself
your soul in dismay

daunting daybreak
illuminate my mind
exposes my heart
leaves me behind
two magnets eternal
conceded by one
lost in translation
seen by the blind
moon newly waxing
the wide world at its prime
fate is ever changing
lost in this imagination I cry

hey nomad
haven't heard from you in a while
how have you been
this mask I wear doesn't feel good anymore
but I know i'm not safe here
you don't take a stand
when i'm the one on blast
you wear your mask deep within
this act is up for me
no chivalry
no belief in beauty or gentle
no iris at the break of dawn
this act halting the show
there's no space on this stage for me
no space in the story you wrote

open book I am
the narrative in your hands
you read the page
but you don't understand

soul on my sleeve
I pour out everything
everything that I am
everything that I was
everything that I will be
see me as I am
see me for what I don't see
bring peace to the unseen
rather than eyes
love through understanding
rather than reprimand
i'm scared of softness
coming from a man
how could you take me as I am
i'll never understand
scared of something I don't know
scared that peace is a lie
your healing softness
still unfathomable when I overthink
allowing me to surrender
helping me learn to stand

my muse
my rival
my waking thought
toxic fuel for my survival
I thrive with you
the thought of you
complimenting my style
I want an us
but there is no us
my thoughts put me on trial
my identity
is following me
cannot act guile
I want to exist
beyond this
be understood without a file

setting sun

moon rising above

what do either of us know about love

what it feels like to show

what it feels like to fade away

looking for something made to stay

just as the sun rises above

and sets every day

my mirror

my reflection

as constant as these glistening waves

I pray we learn not to fight

these ever changing tides

and breathe knowing everything is safe

this ocean

this sun

this moon

the only things certain and true

hope to share this certainty I have with you

my joy
just the one for me
only follow where you lead
you are the happiness of my dreams
swimming through the hallways of your mind
unsure what i'm looking to find
I see a light shining at the bottom of the sea
at depths beyond where i'm used to being
no fear of the depths below
no refusal to face the unknown
where you go is where I go
who held up broken glass to look through
and proclaimed it was you
I'll hold this mirror to reflect the happiness that is true
with the joy you bring me it's the least I can do
we can learn to float
in the rippling joy that surrounds our boat

build me a mansion on the moon
i'll make it a home for you
blue shutters and daisies ready to bloom
no sleepless nights of uncertainty
a door open for eternity
shadows illuminated by light
a dream that doesn't require a fight
for in this house
the fear of an impending doom
has no room
nothing could ever change
the love I have for you

door to freedom within your eyes
key to surrender control of the mind
hold me close
as to see beyond its lies
open door as open as these hearts
for no mind can be truly free
without hearts closeness
surrender to softness
understanding
what it means to simply be

the boat you create
how it keeps me safe
in this wide open sea
it sets me free
free to surrender
free to set down swords
the art of surrendering
seldom lacking care
just being guided by the breeze
hands gently holding the helm
moving forward with what's there
no shame when i'm held by your kind eyes
the shame i've felt for holding on too tight
the shame i've felt for putting up a fight
these swords now oars to our boat
guiding us to our dreams
dreams of a land more concrete
dreams we know we can achieve
we have the key to this salvation we seek
no more dissonance
thinking things are not what they seem
when minds stray
lost in a fog and can hardly see
reaching for swords to keep at bay
let your arms find me
guide me to your soft eyes
in that unadorned sanctuary
we remember everything is okay

you will be back
I will be back
ever so lonely
that we can agree
different upbringings
but you're just like me
lost souls from the youth
we will be free

overflowing cup
it's always been enough
never diamond in the rough
sparkling clear as day
upon a proud hand
hard to see in a hesitant stance
blind we go to the gods and pray
what can we do to stay
in this holy grail
in this love honest and true
out of harm's way
words that assure
rather than presume
through the simple and overlooked
we make the room
for an open door
to this overflowing cup

don't underestimate the power
of a vindictive man
for his power resides
in control and authority
fostered over centuries of time
generations of grasping
whatever he demands
this power
their prized possession
keeps them unable to understand
the true power
they could hold in their hands
he will learn your heart
learn your vulnerabilities
and you become his prey
the first time you say no
the first time you don't stay
he will make sure you can never get away
when will men stop
burning women at the stake
for simply showing them truth
they can't understand

being together
as easy as breathing air
don't worry anymore
we don't have to stay here
heads in the ether
through interlocked hands
we find common ground
not through piercing the atmosphere
just by looking down
seeing our hands have been there
finger in finger
all along

a hand that once held
a hand that once tend
if you weren't ready
why stay in my sacred land
seeing an earth and sun orbit
of my tending of love and an optimistic man
these hands were honored to hold that space
but you haven't been waiting for the one to wait
you've been waiting for someone
who will never hold up a mirror
to your soul
they say eyes are a window to the soul
is that why you couldn't look me in the eyes
couldn't look at my face
as you spoke words of hate
and walked away
these eyes now see every act
an act of violence
upon my heart
forgive me for having enough

running along this river
my gaze meets the ocean
wild wind scathing
my unweathered face
hidden behind
wind broken around your shadow
faced with my own unknown
looming beyond the facade
of the sun's rays
I fear now that we're here
you'll find my depth
too much to share
are we victors of this river
or has its current been tamed
through strength
what will this wild sea believe
is truth duality
for without this wild wind
the sail will fail
so with sureness we look to the horizon each day
trusting that through this ballast and breeze
our journey is safe

I wish I said no
to those who call their friends
other names
names that voice jealousy
words that seek to defame
if I only knew
those friends
would do the same to me
friends who didn't go to their birthday
or christmas
without a gift
friends who always got the invitation
friends who were met with understanding
when their own will became displaced
no amount of security
makes those connections worth the chase

true colors

show me your truth

what does color mean to you

will showing true color always mean something to lose

or can it be freedom from a limited life

the art of me is kind

the art of me is blind

blind in thinking I can be undefined

in this world where people can only find

color through association

justice on my mind

wondering where I should have drew the line

my heart always painting lines in watercolor

this time I'm defining for myself

would I rather dip my brush

in a community of reflections

or embrace a full aura of color

of my own

dear rainbow fish i've been stuck in your pond

this time i'm embracing a wide open ocean

truthful and beautiful mirror

embraces me and shifting tides

meadow covered in snow
what do I truly know
only known is what the archived letter
still evoked
the way it took hold
of every tendon and every bone
every piece of my battered soul
pure resurrection
the way I feel you squeeze my hand
when I feel lost and alone
oh my winged protection
my galahad of the grail
your truest form so holy
becoming convinced you're a ghost
but you're right here
patient immortal meadow
teach me your ways
teach me trust in the everchanging
teach me joy in the stable and slow
take me under your wing
present and alive and inspiring
seeing no difference in the laye
through rain
through leaves
through snow
will I ever know this meadow
without your hand to hold

oh where is your blue beard

is it imagined or is it there

things would be so much easier

if I could hold on to fear

all I see is that same indigo hue

obscure undefinable color

indigo like an iris delivered

by a knight on a stag

my saturn residing in the deepest part of your mind

inner predator and inner prey

why let them play the game

I always feel

like I have to stay

a flower blooms
as the new day rises
full moon at its peak
wondering what you will say
seeking words holy
with no regret
truths felt
yet unknown
from moving lips
words tender
thoughtful in the way they touch
my heart deeply needing
your sentiment of hope
for a future flower bloom
for a future you see me
growing with you
two stems dancing in the wind
meeting at the lips
feeling long awaited lightness
of a true love's kiss

oh how I love the trees

protecting me

from excess rain

shielding me from piercing light

illuminating unnecessary things

branches reaching high above my humble floor

at peace because i'm safe and nothing more

safe to grow without expectation

safe to show my full bloom

safe to close when I need

never pondering what comes after

or what came before

simply in wonder of the trees

truly they're the same as me

seeking stable ground to place roots

growing safe and supported

to experience simple wonder

shell cracked open wide
never intending to be a disguise
these words of mine
shared with you
figuring out what I have to lose
my mind my sacred space
with a room and bed saved just for you
my heart fluffs the pillows and cooks you food
cautious nerves build up doors and gates
a part of me so consumed
wondering if you'll keep my home safe
two doors opening and shutting
flickering like candlelight till they collide
let's tear them down
starting on the same level
of our hands and knees
with tools we know how to use
because I know that's what love is meant to do

california on my mind
land of lost dreams
dreams that weren't what they seemed
something holds me from going back
I was meant to find a new california
there's a sadness that's certain
crying on the fire escape
looking at a beautiful view
of venice boulevard
realizing it's not what you really want
long distance lovers
one way or another
both of you would play cooler
when you're already brighter
than the brightest stars
being yourself isn't actually hard
i'm scared that you see this
as something to win or lose
i've heard the fight was over
if you really choose

pick me up
not because I can't walk
or speak for myself
lift me up to grab the little dipper
to scoop up all the stars
the lost dreams
the unknown terrain
no opportunities missed
or seeked out in vain
for once it's so thrilling
seeing the map of this life
through the sky's eyes
a life I live with you
could never be anything but true
true to my heart
true to my mind
truth that I have yet to know
hidden in plain sight
revealed through
the moons careful tides

I have to remind myself
that you asked me to give up
all the times
you knew I was waiting for you
on the balcony
and you didn't show up
I have to remind myself
because it's so easy
to fall at your feet
and let your tears
rain down on me
I have to remind myself
because the love still lives in me
but you knew the way I love
meant deep change
real release
romeo romeo
wherefore art thou romeo
don't you know
the only thing to deny
was living in vain
don't you know
only love and death
change all things

show me how to stay
show me what love is
what it is to you
who am I to tell you what it means
if love is truth
i'll proclaim at the top of my lungs
that deep love truthfully scares me
and makes me want to run away
it's beyond deep love
it's everything I face
all novelty replaced with old truths
chasing me out
before I can find out what's safe
i'm a phony
a real phony
you weren't ever wrong
for being skeptical of me
for i'm confused by myself
and yet this one truth I face
willingly again and again
letting gravity pull me back
into your embrace
where I'll have to face my truths
face deep love
held too close in your gaze
in your reflection
to be a phony
or escape myself

words left hanging
lost in a liminal space
of forgotten hope
discarded without a trace
a space to sit and wait
hoping and longing
for something to change
waiting to see a soft smile
and vulnerable confessions
as an open heart
and not as chains
wondering where must you go
to find that imagined place
so far away it feels like a dream
but it's right within your heart
in the palm of your hand
finding through interlocked hands
with someone from the same land
there's nothing but free rein

this wildfire ablaze
can only take away
those who would never stay
those who can't stay for themselves
online consumption without real connection
alcohol and special k
do they know how long you've been out of your body
how long your truth has been locked away
how many times you've hit rock bottom
and still can't escape
if you point fingers of blame forever
they will see you wrote your story
when it's always the same
never able to admit you're just afraid
are you afraid they'll see all your colors
your pink, violet, and indigo blue
your deep and all consuming reds
that hold power over you
your browns and grays and murky
those colors so beautiful and valid too
the shadow once was only there
when the sun would shine a certain way
one day that changed
one day it was decided
anyone who could see the shadow
couldn't have space
when you just wanted to escape it without a trace
you can't dance yourself away

on the other side of the glass
you will always see
a woman touching the earth
there was no fantasy
maybe only slight naïveté
just taking a chance
growing something wild and unruly
i'm not even twenty three
and innocent love still has meaning to me
my hard soil suddenly began to soften
innocent love was what I was led to believe
I dreamt of being free
but the solid earth
fell through my hands like sand
my love and desires
were never obscure or unworldly
or hard to understand
It takes two to sow
I saw a farmer and a handyman
but it was new land
and some don't look up to heaven
and see the earth's reflection
the soil turned dry and weary
and it was blamed on the plant
you wanted fruit and trees
but a woman's roots can only grow deep
in land that's loved
not abandoned

I don't have black hair anymore
but I can see why it's easier to remember me that way
because back then I couldn't express my softness
reticent shadow in crowded rooms
that version of me is easier to betray
some days I wake with a newfound kindness
and other days i'm met with people watching my every move with critical eyes
what will I do next
to be a woman is to perform
where are my bouquets of roses
at the end of this show
I'll tell you what I'll do
my character will stop
at the stage edge
I can't be with those
whose character overflows
life becoming the show
the truth of the self can't be defined by hair
shaving of the head won't make one a teacher of god
black hair doesn't make one harsh and goth
those physical things are only a reflection
of feelings or intention
real change happens beneath appearance
beyond the restriction of desired approval
beyond bouquets of roses and applause
It happens through thoughtful actions
and assuming form

faithful siren in me
she holds out for change in weather
because she loves every phase
and knows precisely when
the sun will come out from the shade
she cherishes lost boys
they're not living a lie
we all want to be lost
when this reality is not living
between two pillars I stand
with a truth hard to fathom
truth that there's no difference
between boy and man
fateful mysteries of the sirens demands
you'll only find out by taking her hand
immortal kiss of life to the one
who can bow in the face of his disguise
it's strange what desire
will make boys and men do

bring me your air
how it feeds my fire
inspiration and liberation
through the flame of desire
words rolling off your tongue
underestimated yet superpowers
let our lips meet
as a waterfall meets the lake
overflowing and bursting with sound
never stagnant
always renowned
always embracing a new truth to be told
declarations of love to be shared
simply being held
like the lake holds the waterfall
never taking yet always open
offering a soft place to land
with dedication to being tender and fair

there once was a day

where people waited for love

those no longer wait

because eyes feel they know

all of the wheels' courses

just looking at their plate

can we ever feel truly safe in that illusion

is being safe only knowing what to expect

and what is expected of us

who plated this poison

we have surpassed not waiting

we don't even pursue

how limited this life has become

the biggest love and passion

held in a soundscape

why speak of love

why paint love

why portray love

while touching the world with hate

if life imitates art

then these works must all be fake

god I wanted to experience a river

but even the lake has run dry

I am so sick but I still stand

standing on the edge of the highest cliff

looking at a sunset filled of unexplored color

the sun generously pouring light onto untouched land

I know that I will never know the sacred art of this life

some stories I no longer want to explain
because people expect
men to tell lies
and hold another's love in vain
so the finger of blame
will still point my way
all because I was naive
and believed
when I should have known better
with everyone pumping out a message
like pollution
a message not to open your heart
what is that message helping us achieve

you are my truth
my love
and I hope I can believe you
when you say i'm yours too
because that scares me the most
not being able to accept
a loving and peaceful truth

seven chalices of envisionment

brutal metamorphosis

into two portals of endless abundance

so grounded in the earth

even while lacking true form

your paper doll

has pain of her own

yet she tries on imaginary clothes

seeing potential for growth

because she believes

she can at least own her innocence

i'm proud that I can live aligned with my dreams

look my dreams in the eye

strength no matter the strain

because actions that reflect honest feelings

are what hold value

and birth deep change

my king of coins

the world bows at your name

does life have meaning

beyond that monopoly and fame

I enter the race to show you the abundance of security

that exists beyond paper dolls

beyond defensive ploys

beyond relationships having to be a game

the moon and tower no longer

have to have power or control the reins

in the true security and safety of a lovers embrace

I made sure
you didn't forget her sweatshirt
before you had to leave
because somewhere deep in my soul
I knew you still had to grieve
and to be a friend is to be patient
to show up even when you don't understand
pain always finds its mirror
do you stop and stare
or hold out an open hand
my planets and stars
will always live in your moon
can it be a compassionate home
having someone truly see you
can you honor your waves
can you honor your two faces
and what they have to say
both twins are my friend
with one foot on land
and one foot in the sea
let a door unlock forever
with no need for a key

i'm going to pack up your things
into the boxes you built for me
I don't know if they have real value to sell
I don't know how long I'll keep them close
i'm not bitter
and I'm not trying to be cruel
when I say
I just can't help you
get out of that box anymore

when I first saw your face
I had to do a double take
I knew you
you knew me
our eyes locking gaze
in a room where faces
are meant to be replaced
you've always held on tight
thinking I'd be one to run away
i'm always running somewhere
but you are too
two souls on the path of the five
nothing fake or in disguise
the uncertainty is just change
neither of us are meant to be
locked in a cage
i've always felt with you
that being on the run
has more of a scenic view
I see things from the air
you see things from the ground
it helps me understand
helps me slow down
see love from a different lens

there's a chill that has become familiar
waiting for you up here
stop telling me to come to the ground
don't you know i'm a lady bird
i'm a phoenix trying to recover her wings
up in the clouds
I have a music box unwinding
It won't wait to unravel
but it may work better
with the help of a knight on a black steed
a knight ready to learn of true abundance
in order to become a king
climb up this tower
and we descend down together
saturn is my enemy and my friend
a thousand years unfold
what remains is a single memory of a face
with a stare that turns
this lady bird into a flame
the best thing about wings
is being able to touch the sky
and fly to touch the earth below
I feel love by being free
freedom can be shared
that's how I want things to be

I want to move on
I was there when you were just falling behind
but that turned into vindication and lies
my eyes no longer yearn
for a subtle kiss that no one sees
i've jumped over the city walls
on a trampoline
and now they've banned me
the things I don't mind
have had some blurry lines
the mark of my acceptance was never too high
every day I saw a rising sun
as much as I wish for you to shine
I can't go on just reading your mind
love should be seen
I have to forgive myself for getting used to the dark

try to swim upstream
on the river of death
dear estranged lover
you never tried
to break the pattern
last night I cried
tears of contentment
is life really easier in a disguise
my life is with the sun
in it's light
I see both brightness and shadows
in the abyss with the absence of light
nothing can be illuminated
nothing can be reflected
from one thing to another
must I continue
to pay my dues
with half of the seasons
let my mind be free from your singing
that song has played too long

last year on a blue moon
there was hope
hidden in plain sight
in a rare beatles vinyl
that night was magic
but you watched the shooting star
cross the sky
without making a wish
i've always believed in love
maybe at one point you did

I never thought it would be a possibility
to have ivy of two pairs of eyes
growing all over me
can home with another
ever be safe
I can't escape this fire ablaze
I can't escape this desire
i've started to become a widow
aging from waiting
for support from the vines
will they lift me to the sky
or keep me confined
i'm finding I have my foot in the door
of two homes at the same time
all I know is right now it feels safer
to step into the door that's wide open
i'm exhausted from worrying about keys
and being locked out
unexpectedly

it's dangerous how much you feel like home
a home i don't yet know
a home that takes me so far away
is it figment or is it fate
am I meant to take the leap of faith
to journey where angels fear to tread
do I have what it takes
is it safe
to put my heart above my head
this self undoing
brings me closer to myself
and closer to you
to lie in my own inner conviction
would be laying in a premature grave
I save myself when I grasp this truth
the truth a sharpened stake
stabbing me with its blade
hoping in return I save you too
I wince in a liberating haze
envisioning you opening up your heart
becoming two wise fools rushing in
finding the peace in this home
we haven't yet known

Printed in the USA
CPSIA information can be obtained
at www.ICGtesting.com
CBHW042136251024
16243CB00113B/87

9 798991 452908